To my dad,
Lloyd Blonder,
who always said
I should be a writer.
~R.B.~

To loving parents
everywhere.
~H.Y.~

into your Dreams

by
Roger Blonder

illustrations by
Hedy Yudaw

ObservaStory™ Books

Not
yellow-purple
polka-dot

or standing
on your head
time!

It's time to brush your teeth, ★ ★ read a story, tuck you in.

Time to wander in your thoughts

throughout the kind of day it's been.

Time to drift away in sleep
to a land of dreams
where you can keep...

a pet hippo
named **Harpo**
who should learn to use a spoon!

or a strumming fuzzy **wuzzlebee**

who hums a happy tune.

Where you can live in a castle
made of yellow sliced cheese ~

or soar with a panda on a flying trapeze ~

Where you can play shuffleboard
with a skydiving gourd

drink chocolate pudding
with an aardvark named Sven ~

go fishing with llamas in chartreuse pajamas
or share sips of cider with a finely dressed wren.

Where you can swing like a monkey
in the branches of the trees

or frolic on a dolphin
in the waves 'cross the seas.

Catch a ride on a lark
who will fly you to a park ~

Where your toys are your friends
and the fun never ends!

You can lick every flavor
in the ice-cream store!

You can do all of this
in your dreams ~ and more!

But first you'll need to do one thing
of which the time has come for me to sing.

Time to lie down in your bed.

Time to rest your little head.

Not time to shout.

No need to weep.

The time has come to go to sleep.

Not climb a chair, or brush your hair,

or play with blocks,

or put on socks ~

But time for soothing quiet sounds –
not revving ups,
but calming downs
from all the fun we had today.

Tomorrow there's more time to play.

But now it's time to rest your head.

Time to lie down in your bed.

Time to take one final look.

Time to close
the bedtime book

and then your eyes,

with final sighs,

as this old day

just slips away...

Book design and art direction by Roger Blonder
Illustration by Hedy Yudaw with Roger Blonder
Text set in Cabrito Didone

ObservaStory™ Books
Calabasas, CA 91302

www.observastory.com

First Paperback Edition

Made in the USA
San Bernardino, CA
19 September 2018